NICK CAVE & THE BAD SEEDS

· ·

PUSH THE SKY AWAY

T0039700

HAL•LEONARD®

We No Who U R

Words by Nick Cave

Music by Nick Cave & Warren Ellis

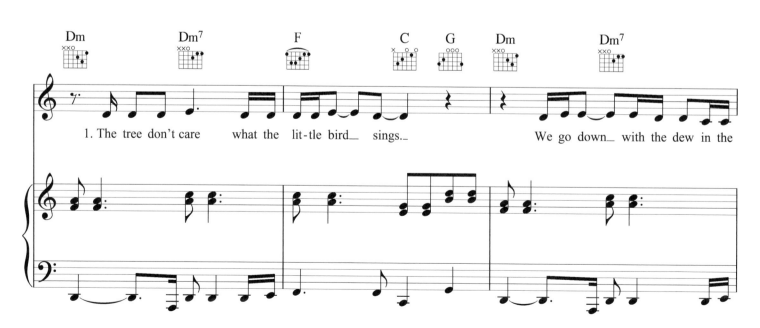

1. The tree don't care what the lit-tle bird_ sings._ We go down_ with the dew in the

6

Wide Lovely Eyes

Words by Nick Cave
Music by Nick Cave & Warren Ellis

land - ing.___ All a-mong the myths_ and the le-gends we cre - ate and

all the laugh-ing sto - ries we tell our friends.___ Close the win-dows, clear up the

mess it's get-ting late.___ It's dark - er and clos - er to the end.___

Through the tun - nel___ and down to the sea.

10

Water's Edge

Words by Nick Cave
Music by Nick Cave, Warren Ellis & Thomas Wydler

Go way down where the stones meet the

water's edge shaking their asses.

sea.

And all

Freely ♩. = 56

Am   G

____ you young girls,   where do you hide?

      2° lov - ers

Down by the wat-er____ and the rest-less tide.

a tempo ♩. = 68

N.C.

2. And the local boys hide on the
4. With a bible of tricks they do with

mound and watch.
their legs the girls Reaching for the speech
reach for the speech

15

5. Their

legs   wide   to   the world   like   bibles   open

19

world.　　　　　　And,

God　　　knows,　　　　the　　local　　boys.

It's　　　the

Jubilee Street

Words by Nick Cave
Music by Nick Cave & Warren Ellis

1. On Ju-bi-lee Street there was a girl named Bee.
2. The prob-lem was she had a lit-tle black book.

of love up Ju-bi-lee Street. Oh look at me now. 2° I'm fly-ing.

I'm glow-ing, I'm fly - ing. Look at me now.

Look at me now.

To Coda ⊕

D.S. al Coda

⊕ *Coda*

Repeat ad lib. to fade

Mermaids

Words by Nick Cave
Music by Nick Cave & Warren Ellis

We Real Cool

Words by Nick Cave
Music by Nick Cave & Warren Ellis

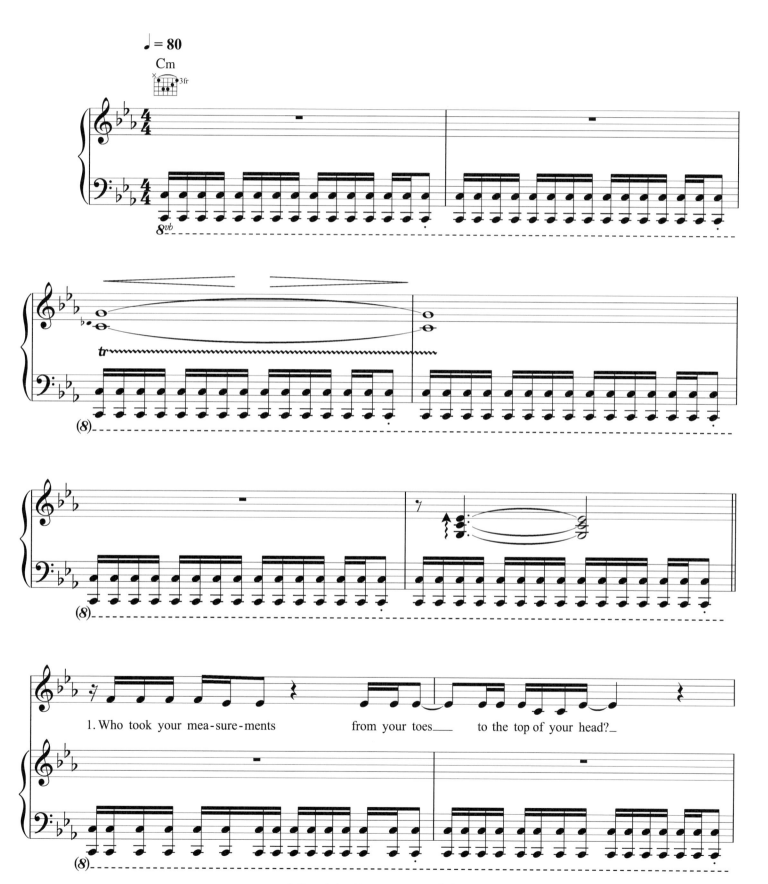

1. Who took your mea-sure-ments from your toes___ to the top of your head?___

round-ing up the kids for their meal?__ Who chased your shad-ow run-ning out be-hind?__

__ Cling-ing to your high fly-ing heels. Your high

fly-ing, high__ fly-ing,__ high__ fly-ing heels. Who

was it? Yeah, you know we real cool. On the
2° And the

far side of the morn-ing.
world keeps on turn-ing.

Who was it? Yeah, you know___ we real

cool.

And I hope___you're list-'ning,

To Coda ⊕

are you?

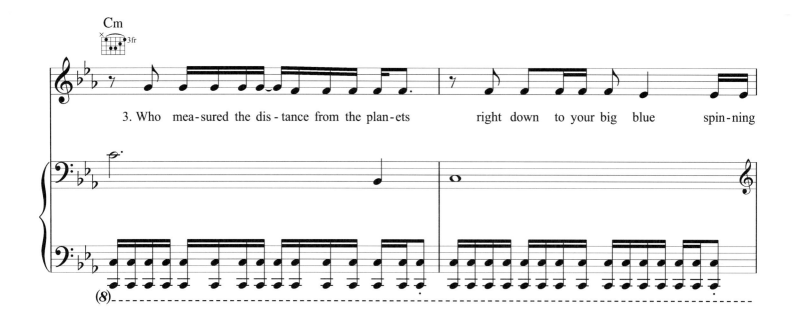

3. Who mea-sured the dis-tance from the plan-ets right down to your big blue spin-ning

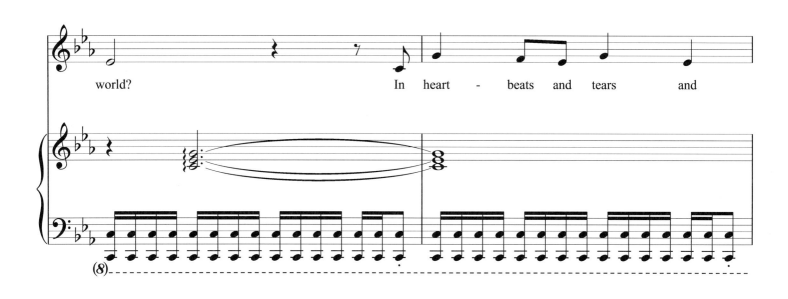

world? In heart - beats and tears and

ner - vous laugh - ter spill-ing down_ all o-ver you, girl. Who

D.S. al Coda

Si - ri - us   is   eight - point - six___ light   years_ a - way.

Arc - tur - us___   is   thir - ty   sev - en.

The past   is the past___   and it's___   here_____ to stay.___

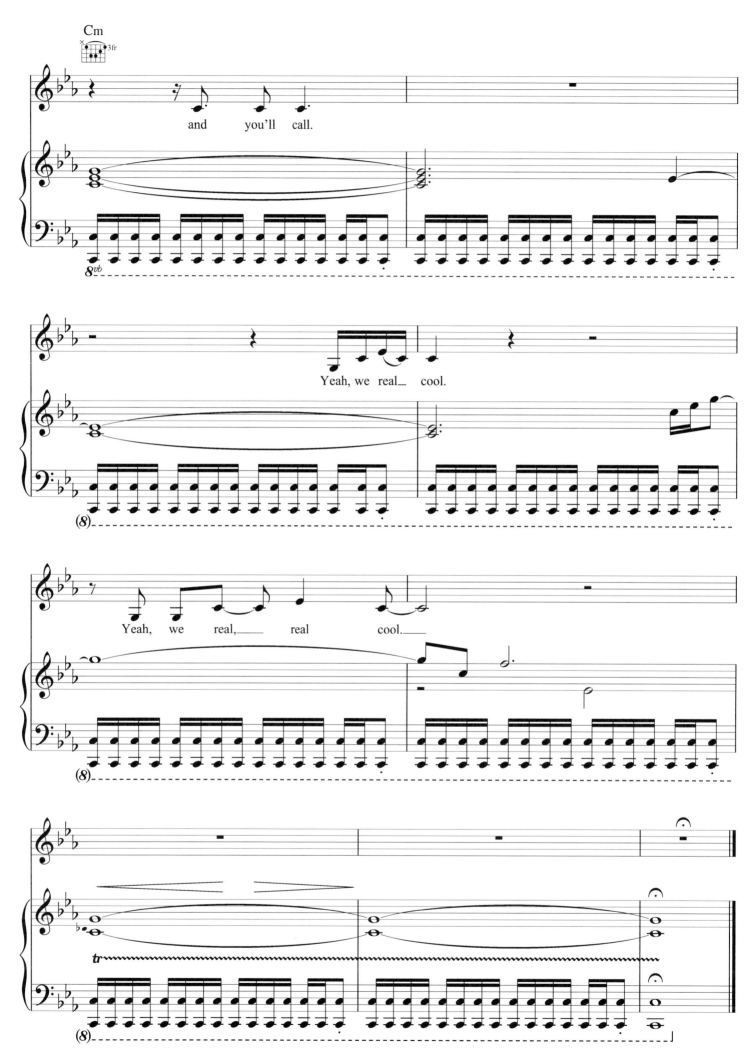

and you'll call.

Yeah, we real__ cool.

Yeah, we real,_____ real cool._____

Finishing Jubilee Street

Words by Nick Cave
Music by Nick Cave, Warren Ellis & Thomas Wydler

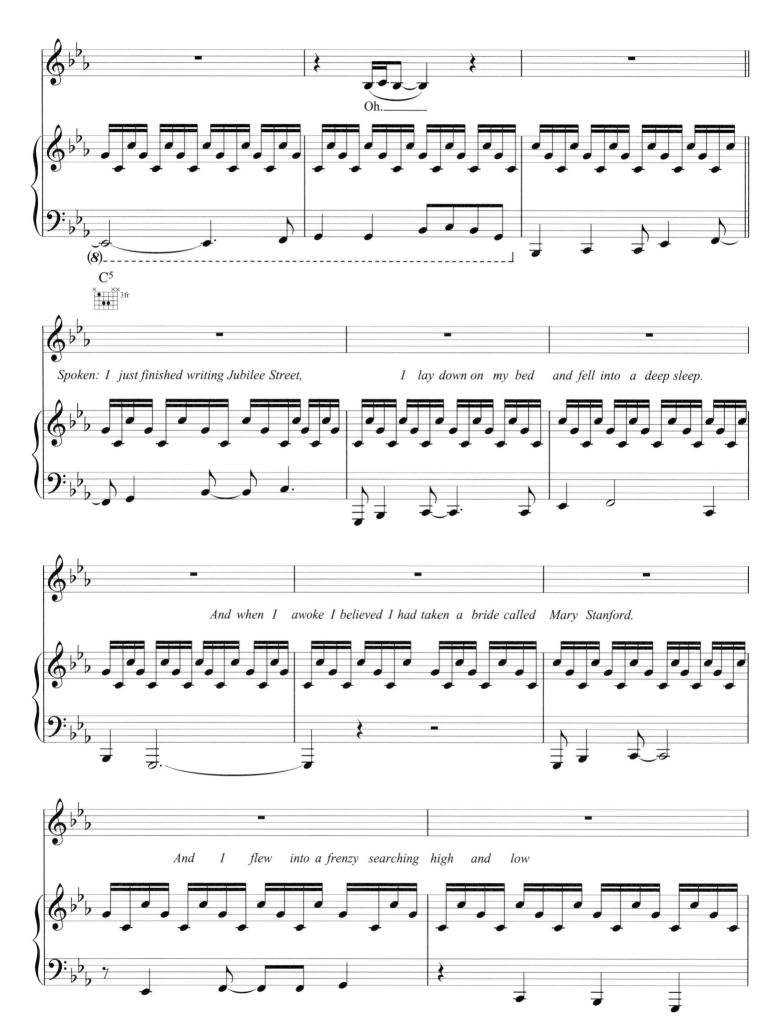

Oh.

C5

Spoken: I just finished writing Jubilee Street,   I lay down on my bed   and fell into a deep sleep.

And when I   awoke I believed I had taken a bride called   Mary Stanford.

And   I   flew   into a frenzy searching high   and   low

because in my dream the girl was very young.   Oh.   I said__

hey lit - tle girl,__   where do you hide?__

You draw light - ning   from the sky.__

Oh.__

com- in' on___ down,___ com- in' on___ down.___

Last night your shadow scampered up the wall   it fly

and leaped like a black spider between your legs and cried.

47

See that girl___ com- in' on___ down,___

com- in' on___ down,___ com- in' on___ down.___

Repeat to fade

49

Higgs Boson Blues

Words by Nick Cave
Music by Nick Cave & Warren Ellis

Can't re-
He got the
-al jaw.
And with a mum-mi-fied

-mem-ber a-ny-thing at all.____
real kill-er groove.
cat
But I'm driv-ing my car____
Rob-ert John-son and the dev-il, man.
and a cone-like hat
that the

____ down____ to Ge-ne-va.
Don't know who's gon-na rip off who.
Cal -i-phate forced on the Jews.____

A(sus4)
G
Bm

I've_____ been sit-ting in my____ base-ment pa-ti-o._____
Driv-ing my car. Flame trees on fire.
Oh, can you feel my heart beat? Can you feel my

heart beat?

It was_____ hot. Up a-bove
Sit-ting and sing-ing the Higgs Bo-son Blues._____

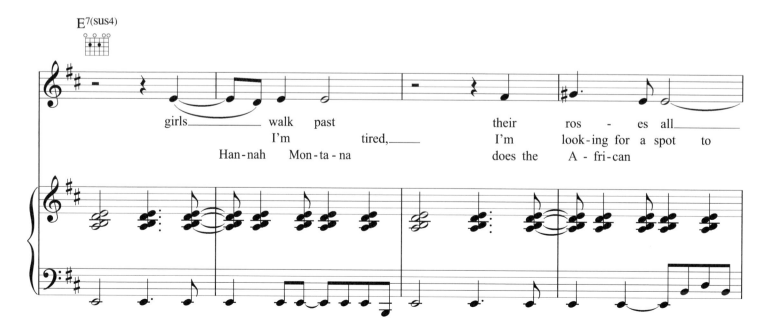

girls_____ walk past their ros - es all_____
I'm tired,_____ I'm look-ing for a spot to
Han-nah Mon-ta-na does the A - fri-can

Oh let the damn day break.

Rain- y days al - ways make me sad.

Push The Sky Away

Words by Nick Cave
Music by Nick Cave & Warren Ellis

Published by
Hal Leonard

Exclusive Distributors:
Hal Leonard
7777 West Bluemound Road, Milwaukee, WI 53213
Email: info@halleonard.com

Hal Leonard Europe Limited
42 Wigmore Street Marylebone, London, WIU 2 RY
Email: info@halleonardeurope.com

Hal Leonard Australia Pty. Ltd.
4 Lentara Court Cheltenham, Victoria 9132, Australia
Email: info@halleonard.com.au

Order No. AM1006522
ISBN: 978-1-78305-107-6
This book © Copyright 2013 Hal Leonard

Edited by Jenni Norey.
Music arranged by Derek Jones.
Music processed by Paul Ewers Music Design.

Cover photo by Dominique Issermann.
Original design by Tom Hingston Studio.

Printed in the EU

www.halleonard.com